BITCOIN

The Mystery of Satoshi Nakamoto

EPIPHANY HUB PRINTS

BITCOIN

COPYRIGHT © [2023] BY [EPIPHANY HUB PRINTS]

The emergence of Bitcoin signaled a paradigm shift in the financial industry, with far-reaching philosophical, technological, and economic ramifications.

TABLE OF CONTENT

INTRODUCTION

Within the mysterious domains of the digital age, a ground-breaking idea called Bitcoin first surfaced in 2009, upending the established financial system and igniting a worldwide obsession. Bitcoin, the creation of the mysterious persona known only as Satoshi Nakamoto, challenged preconceived ideas about money and transactions by introducing the world to the idea of decentralized digital currency.

A document titled "Bitcoin: A Peer-to-Peer Electronic Cash System," written by the pseudonymous Satoshi Nakamoto, describes the complex inner workings of this cutting-edge cryptocurrency. Still, one of the most fascinating mysteries of the twenty-first century is the identity of the real Nakamoto. Thoughts and conjecture abound, the author's pseudonym endures, veiled in secrecy and purposeful obfuscation.

The distributed ledger technology used by Bitcoin, known as a blockchain, guarantees immutability, security, and transparency. Due to its decentralized structure, people have more influence over their financial activities and no longer require middlemen like banks. The 21 million bitcoin supply is restricted, and mining—which verifies transactions and produces new coins—adds levels of complexity to the ecosystem surrounding this virtual currency.

As Bitcoin gained traction, its value skyrocketed, drawing in supporters as well as detractors. Its ramifications were debated by governments and financial institutions, and its development was further shaped by a thriving community of fans and developers.

The history of Bitcoin, from its enigmatic beginnings to its present position as a widely used financial instrument, is evidence of the revolutionary potential of decentralized technology to completely alter the nature of money and finance in the future.

To Investors,

The Winklevoss brothers, Cameron and Tyler, are guest bloggers today. They have long been Ethereum and Bitcoin investors. Additionally, they are the creators of Gemini, one of the top bitcoin exchanges in the US.

SUMMARY

From a small movement of cryptographers, computer scientists, and cypherpunks, Bitcoin has become a more and more common phenomen. It is beginning to compel a restructuring of the global financial system, and its implications for philosophy, technology, and the economy are only growing. An overview of the historical and cultural relevance of bitcoin is given in this article.

BITCOIN'S PREDECESSORS

As we have come to know these terms, Bitcoin is the first cryptocurrency in the world. The term "Bitcoin" (uppercase "B") designates the native digital asset token of the Bitcoin network, which is a peer-to-peer network that keeps track of ownership of all bitcoins (lowercase "b") through a decentralized public ledger known as the "BLOCKCHAIN."

Apart from establishing digital currency devoid of trust, Bitcoin has also sparked a push to disperse the current centralized financial services. However, there had been prior attempts to create digital currency before Bitcoin. It is difficult to conceive that it would have been successful if not for the lessons learned and concepts put forth in these earlier endeavors, as it was built upon the shoulders of giants that came before it.

Nick Szabo is credited for conceptualizing the idea of scarcity in relation to digital currency when he introduced Bit Gold in 1998 and later discussed it on his blog. Szabo is a computer scientist and a founding member of the Cypherpunks, an avant-garde organization of technologists committed to advancing privacy via electronic money and encryption. Having come together in the 1980s, the Cypherpunks discussed a wide range of subjects pertaining to censorship, economics, and cryptography on a frequent basis via the Cypherpunks mailing list. The philosophy of the Cypherpunk movement was encapsulated in the 1993 publication A Cypherpunk's Manifesto, written by mathematician Eric Hughes, Timothy C. May, and John Gilmore.

"Precious metals and collectibles have an unforgettably scarcity due to the costliness of their creation," Szabo observed in the late 1990s. Thus, his goal was to develop a protocol "that would enable the creation of irreversibly expensive bits online with little reliance on reliable third parties."

Now introduce Bit Gold. A computer (Alice) would have to expend resources to solve a proof of work (PoW) puzzle that would generate a PoW chain in order to attempt to impose "cost" centered on the establishment of property on a decentralized public registry. Alice's freshly formed property has a theoretical value that increases with the length of the chain. This was a digital equivalent of the labor (i.e., energy) needed to extract gold from the earth.

Alice's non-fungible chain would be uploaded to the distributed public registry and she would receive Bit Gold in exchange if her proof-of-work chain was approved and confirmed by the majority of the network's computers, or nodes, a process known as attaining consensus.

The registry eliminated the possibility of a user spending the same Bit Gold more than once by allowing any node to quickly and easily verify Bit Gold Alice's ownership cryptographically. However, the inadequacy of the Bit Gold consensus mechanism stemmed from the low cost at which a malicious actor could fabricate a large number of nodes (referred to as "sybills") and manipulate the property register (a process known as a "Sybil attack").

The network would become increasingly centralized and the approved nodes would have an excessive amount of power if Bit Gold tried to prevent this by restricting the number of nodes that could take part in managing the property registry.

Around the same time as Bit Gold, B-Money also emerged as a rival to Bitcoin. It is mentioned in the Bitcoin whitepaper and was put out by computer engineer, cryptographer, and cypherpunk Wei Dai. An "anonymous, distributed electronic cash system" was the idea behind B-Money. Even though it was never developed past the whitepaper stage, it contained several ideas that eventually found their way into Bitcoin and the plethora of other cryptocurrencies that Bitcoin has subsequently inspired. These ideas included a distributed ledger, digital signatures for transactions, and proof-of-work (PoW) money creation (like Bit Gold).

Cynthia Dwork and Moni Naor initially proposed the concept of incorporating cost (or digital scarcity) into a proof-of-work system in 1993 as a defense against abuses like spam. This idea was used by Dr. Adam Back, an English cypherpunk, into his 1997 project Hashcash, a service designed to reduce spam and denial-of-service attacks. It was (and still is) cheap to send out bulk emails to unwary people.

Therefore, Dr. Back set out to make sending emails more expensive, making the cost prohibitive for abusive users but negligible for honest users. In order to create a Hashcash token, a sender must figure out a PoW problem. This token, which resembles a postage stamp, is delivered to the intended recipient along with an email. The email will be delivered if the token is genuine; if not, it will bounce. The cost of generating a Hashcash token would be insignificant for an ordinary user, but it would be prohibitively expensive for a spammer to manufacture tokens in quantity.

By proving that digital scarcity may be produced even in the midst of abundance, Hashcash opened the eyes of two or more Cypherpunks. Shortly after, Bit Gold's Szabo and B-money's Dai would use the idea of digital scarcity to create money. PoW puzzles are a form of energy that, if used to manufacture coins, would transfer the energy value of those efforts onto the coins themselves.

Another Cypherpunk, Hal Finney, attempted to build a cryptocurrency system called reusable proof of work (RPoW) in 2004 in an attempt to outperform Bit Gold. Finney's Proof-of-Work (RPoW) approach simplified the Bit Gold plan, and it also leveraged Hashcash's Proof-of-Work mechanism to create new coins.

But in order to prevent double-spending, the system sacrificed decentralization for simplicity by depending on a centralized server. It would take an additional five years for Bitcoin to integrate all of the many innovations made by Szabo, Dai, Back, and Finney into a workable, completely decentralized digital currency that is trustless.

ENTER BITCOIN

The first block of the Bitcoin blockchain, known as the "Genesis Block," was mined in January 2009, marking the network's inception. In 2008, the Bitcoin white paper was released. With the help of Bitcoin, a fully decentralized, trustless digital currency was successfully built, removing the need for dependable financial middlemen when sending money between users online.

This was made feasible by a significant advancement in its consensus method, which addressed issues that Bit Gold was unable to completely defend against by utilizing Hashcash PoW. More precisely, the Bitcoin mining process encourages miners to follow the rules and eliminates the need to predetermine the number of nodes.

This is how it functions: Bitcoin depends on the majority of hashrate, or the network's processing power, to reach consensus rather than the majority of nodes, or "miners," to do so. It costs money for a miner to obtain the majority of the network's hashrate, which makes tampering with the ledger costly. Furthermore, by doing this, a dishonest miner would forfeit the generous rewards of freshly created bitcoin (referred to as the "block reward"), which are given out to the "winning" miner who properly solves the PoW puzzle roughly every ten minutes. As a result, it is presumed that a logical, profit-driven miner will devote her processing power to maintaining the blockchain's integrity rather than attempting to alter it or deceive the system.

For this reason, the Proof of Work (PoW) principle of Hashcash is essential to the creation of new bitcoin (digital scarcity) as well as the protection of the Bitcoin network (expensive to attack, block reward opportunity cost). Once primarily a movement among computer scientists and cryptographers, digital money is now becoming a more widely accepted phenomena thanks to this straightforward yet elegant incentive structure.

THE MYSTERY OF SATOSHI NAKAMOTO

The most fascinating enigma of the last ten years may be who the creator of Bitcoin, Satoshi Nakamoto, actually is. The true identity of Nakamoto has been the subject of much research and conjecture ever since the publication of the Bitcoin whitepaper. Some have even theorized that Nakamoto might not even be a single person, but rather a collection of people working together. All of the aforementioned early digital money pioneers have been falsely accused of being Nakamoto at different times, but they all vehemently contest this.

At least in the beginning, Satoshi probably feared the negative steps that governments may take, which is why he went to tremendous measures to remain anonymous. There were no hints as to Nakamoto's true identity in his or her posts on development platforms, websites, and cryptography forums, and his or her contributions to the development of the Bitcoin Network ceased in the middle of 2010.

After sending an enigmatic note in 2011 that read, "[I've] moved on to other things," Satoshi vanished from the Internet and was never heard from again. As of right now, no solid proof has emerged to identify the person or people who went by Satoshi Nakamoto's pseudonym, or "nym" as the Cypherpunks called it. Nakamoto is still at large as of this writing.

Although Satoshi's identity and location have received a lot of attention, members of the Bitcoin community—often referred to as "Bitcoiners"—think that one of the biggest advantages of Bitcoin is that nobody really knows who Satoshi really is. There is only math and lines of code that speak for themselves; there is no founder, no leader, and no single point of failure. This is entirely consistent with the principles of a decentralized, trustless currency.

Bitcoin's Cultural Significance

The financial crisis of 2007–2008, which was caused by the reckless lending and risk-taking activities of banks worldwide, was a backdrop against which Bitcoin was built. Many banks obtained government bailouts in spite of their hazardous behavior, which sparked massive protests and a general lack of trust in the global financial system.

As a response to the "inherent weaknesses of the trust based model," Bitcoin surfaced. The following message that Nakamoto penned in the Genesis Block of Bitcoin is not by accident: The Times 03/Jan/2009: The chancellor is about to launch a second bank rescue. Many people consider this message to be a call to arms as well as a timestamp.

Decentralization, whose main tenet is the empowerment of the individual, is made feasible by Bitcoin. By its very nature, it returns control to the many instead of the few. Within the next ten years, the principles and architecture of Bitcoin will completely reimagine money, the financial system, and the Internet to provide everyone more freedom, opportunity, and choice. similar to the printing press, personal computer, and early Internet inventions that came before it. And it matters a lot.

THE MARKET MANIPULATORS ARE LAUGHING AS THEY RUIN THE WORLD

To investors,

March, 2020, the global epidemic threw financial markets into a state of extreme unpredictability and volatility. It seemed like a month every day. Every time the market opened, every asset class appeared to be losing more and more ground. Circuit breakers were nearly always tripping, the Federal Reserve was announcing emergency interest rate cuts, and the majority of Wall Street "capitalists" were essentially socialists who begged the government for bailouts.

It was a complete catastrophe, to put it mildly, and nobody thought it would get much worse. At this point, the US government and Federal Reserve decided to step in. As one might anticipate from a Keynesian economic perspective, the market intervention was regarded as a virtue. Indeed, a noble deed. To save the day, the cavalry arrived. and keep investors' pockets full.

Two emergency interest rate reductions to 0% were implemented. The repo markets received extraordinary support and attention worth hundreds of billions of dollars. The lawmakers were addicted to adopting fiscal stimulus laws, which resulted in the injection of trillions of dollars into the economy, much like a heroin addict who needs to hit again before suffering a withdrawal.

The absurd thing was that the heads of the established financial system cheered and showed appreciation for the central banks' and politicians' participation. They asserted that the common people, the tiny people, required aid right away. If not, individuals would be abandoned, put to death, and the institution as a whole might come to an end. Really? You observed them tweeting this absurdity. You watched them on TV discussing it. Additionally, you observed them praising each action and requesting stimulus and bailout funds from the government.

Certain airlines were given free loans worth billions of dollars that were never had to be repaid. PPP loans were taken out by several Wall Street asset management companies. It seemed strange that the wealthiest members of society would advocate for market intervention, don't you think?

Not at all. They were fully aware of what was going to occur. These are thoughtful people. They have a lengthy history in marketplaces. During the global financial crisis, the secret was revealed to the general public. The government and central bank will remove all risk from the market and significantly increase the wealth of anybody holding assets if you can get them to intervene.

Guess what? That is exactly what happened.
The S&P 500 reached an all-time high this past week on the same day that the Federal Reserve's balance sheet reached a record-breaking high of more than $8 trillion. VERY SAME DAY! Just a coincidence? Not in my opinion.

Although the US Treasury Department, Federal Reserve, and government have been manipulating the market for over ten years, they have really stepped it up in the last twelve to fifteen months. The market interventionists did what they did best, lowering the cost of capital to 0% and injecting trillions of dollars into the system, using COVID-19 as an excuse.

The wealth disparity in our current economy is the widest it has ever been. Because most people are making more money from government assistance than they would in the labor market, small business owners are unable to find enough workers to manage their enterprises. Even before the pandemic, there are more available jobs in the US economy than ever before. People genuinely object to returning to their jobs.

Furthermore, in May, inflation reached a five percent rate. Economists and the mainstream media assured us that inflation wouldn't be an issue for the most of last year. They said that because we were in a deflationary period, the market could absorb all further monetary stimulus. However, we are informed that the inflation is just temporary now that it has arrived. In the near to medium future, it will disappear. You shouldn't be concerned!

False. Not a single company that is increasing the cost of its products or services intends to reduce the cost in the future. The concept of temporary inflation does not exist. Prices gradually increase when a currency depreciates. A money that can and will be created indefinitely cannot be made more valuable. You can slow down inflation, but you can't stop it from happening. No changes in monetary policy result in a decrease in the cost of goods and services.

However, this is not just a story about the declining labor force participation rate and rising costs of products. Markets have been completely dehumanized by the Federal Reserve and numerous political administrations. At this point, they have deceived them so well that children are growing up believing that there is no longer any risk in the market. Bear markets are forbidden by the architects of our monetary system.

Market corrections are no longer permitted.

A staggering amount of market intervention and manipulation occurs at the first sign of any reversion to the mean. The endeavor to manipulate the market is more vigorous the stronger the force of correction. The Federal

Reserve and government officials have become so conceited that they were actually boasting about having limitless resources on 60 Minutes. This isn't something you make up.

So where do we go from here?

There is no going back, to put it succinctly. There is no turning back from the extreme manipulation of the market. The government and central bank would find it extremely difficult to let free market forces clean up the mess they've created. It would hurt too much. Every politician would be swapped out. Unrest in society would result. It would quickly become very nasty.

The market manipulators are left with no choice but to carry on with their manipulations. The pretense is now required. The interventionists need to be prepared with more interest rate reduction and monetary stimulus packages each time the market attempts to correct. Why limit yourself to $5 trillion? How come we can't reach $10 trillion? Twenty trinlions?

The absurd aspect is that we will witness everything. The deception we have witnessed over the past 18 months will be nothing compared to what we will witness in the future, whether or not people realize we are racing over a cliff. Over time, the Federal Reserve's balance sheet will continue to expand. The price of assets will keep rising to the moon. You really can be a complete moron and still become wealthy financially.

Simply run out of money. Purchase any asset valued in US dollars, then take a seat and unwind. The dollar will keep losing value as a result of market manipulation, driving up the value of your assets. You'll become wealthier than you ever imagined thanks to them.

Sounds incredible, doesn't it? Regretfully, 45% of Americans in the lowest income bracket have no investable assets. They barely make ends meet. They keep all of their money in US dollars. Therefore, the market manipulators are penalizing the most vulnerable members of our society while simultaneously making asset holders extremely affluent. The impoverished get poorer while the privileged gain richer.

Rich individuals are very reluctant to discuss this dark truth. They are not interested in advocating for the money printer to be turned off in order to narrow the wealth disparity gap. They will discuss the initiatives to demonstrate virtue by paying marginally more wages, among other things. However, they are aware that those actions won't have the structural effect required to reduce the gap and give the bottom 45% of residents more authority.

This is the reason I support bitcoin so strongly. It is the only money that is impervious to depreciation. It is not under the jurisdiction of a central bank or government. The monetary policy is definitive in addition to being certain. There won't be a macroeconomic devaluation. To retain your earned wealth, you don't have to be a seasoned investor or a well-educated individual. All you have to do is accumulate digital currency and watch as your buying power grows over time.

This is the benefit of having a stable monetary policy that is open and programmatic. For billions of people worldwide, Bitcoin is exactly the asset protection they need. The market manipulators are actually waging trillion-dollar marketing campaigns for the real answer to wealth disparity while they are feigning to save the planet.

I hope the proponents of market intervention would stop it. I hope they would allow the free markets carry out their optimal function. I wish they would quit hurting the lowest 45% of Americans who carry cash and artificially increasing asset prices. However, they refuse to. For this reason, we use bitcoin. For this reason, I dedicate my entire day to attempting to inform billions of people worldwide about self-defense against this insanity.

The world is awakening, although slowly. Individuals are starting to recognize the issues. They fail to see why, in a depressed economy, equities are rising. They understand that, at a time when tens of millions of Americans were unemployed and the US economy was all but shut down, it is incomprehensible that the wealthy could have become even wealthier. They've been searching for a solution since they realized something wasn't right.

This explains why bitcoin is taking off so quickly. People are now aware of its significance on a global scale. Allow the manipulators of the market to carry on with their scheme. All they are doing is quickening the inevitable conclusion. I'm hoping for the best for them. Get informed in the interim and impart your expertise to individuals in your vicinity.

Avoid being caught off guard. Holding an asset that is losing value at a historically rapid rate is not a good idea. Make sure you have the safeguards in place to prevent the depreciation of your purchasing power. You earned your money through labor. Don't let the wealthy and powerful to let it wither away.

CONCLUSION

In conclusion, the mystery surrounding Bitcoin's mysterious creator, Satoshi Nakamoto, adds a fascinating dimension to the story of this ground-breaking digital money. When Bitcoin first appeared, the financial world underwent a radical change, upending preconceived ideas about money, centralization, and trust. Because of its decentralized structure and use of blockchain technology, it created a new paradigm in which people could interact directly with one another, eschewing middlemen and taking charge of their own financial independence.

Whether deliberate or not, Satoshi Nakamoto's anonymity personifies the spirit of decentralization, leaving us with a persistent enigma that has captured the interest of both enthusiasts and skeptics. Beyond its explosive price increase, Bitcoin has left a lasting impact by igniting a wider discussion about the nature of money, privacy, and how technology will affect our financial future.

The enigma surrounding Satoshi Nakamoto serves as a reminder of the revolutionary potential inherent in decentralized technology as we navigate the constantly changing cryptocurrency landscape. Whether Nakamoto's identity is finally made public or not, Bitcoin is proof of the ability of innovation to upend well-established structures. The mysterious beginnings of Bitcoin will no doubt continue to spark debates in the years to come regarding openness, trust, and the opportunities that arise when decentralized principles upend the existing quo.

www.ingramcontent.com/pod-product-compliance
Lightning Source LLC
LaVergne TN
LVHW022127060326
832903LV00063B/4796